WILD
WORLD

illustrated by
Hvass&Hannibal

written by
Angela McAllister

WIDE EYED EDITIONS

Dedicated to Bjørn, Bibi, and Olivia —Sofie and Nan Na

For Carolyn, Clive, Tilly, and Natalie —Angela

Brimming with creative inspiration, how-to projects, and useful information to enrich your everyday life, Quarto Knows is a favourite destination for those pursuing their interests and passions. Visit our site and dig deeper with our books into your area of interest: Quarto Creates, Quarto Cooks, Quarto Homes, Quarto Lives, Quarto Drives, Quarto Explores, Quarto Gifts, or Quarto Kids.

Wild World © 2018 Quarto Publishing plc. Text © 2018 Angela McAllister.
Illustrations © 2018 Hvass&Hannibal.
First published in 2018 by Wide Eyed Editions, an imprint of The Quarto Group.
400 First Avenue North, Suite 400, Minneapolis, MN 55401, USA.
T (612) 344-8100 F (612) 344-8692 www.QuartoKnows.com

A catalog record for this book is available from the British Library.

ISBN 978-1-84780-966-7
The illustrations were created digitally
Set in BonvenoCF, Old Standard TT, and Optima

Published by Jenny Broom and Rachel Williams
Designed by Nicola Price
Edited by Katie Cotton
Production by Kate O'Riordan

Manufactured in Dongguan, China TL 112017

9 8 7 6 5 4 3 2 1

Take a journey through the Wild World,

From mountain peak to forest floor,

Through swamp mud and starry pool,

Across golden sand and snowdrift.

Discover why each place is like no other.

Gaze at amazing plants and trees,

The birds, insects,

Reptiles, mammals, and fish

That share this one, beautiful Earth.

But look close, look quick,

For all is changing—

The Wild World is in danger,

Calling with many voices for your care.

What we see may soon be gone.

Learn how to protect it.

There is no time to lose . . .

Rainforest

Hot, wet rain forest
Spreads a green roof high above the earth,
Loud with the swing, swoop, and song of life.
Bright *birds* flash,
Apes chatter,
Plump fruit ripens to slowly tempt the *sloth*.
But what is hidden below that canopy, where the sun cannot pass?
A shady world
Of strangle vines scrambling for a shaft of light,
Lush leaves searching for a glimmer in the gloom.
Haunt of mighty *gorilla*, poisonous *frog*,
And slithering *python*.
A secret world
Where fungi glow upon tree roots,
Termites swarm among dead things on the dark forest floor,
Never knowing that their tiny work feeds giants.

Arctic

Cold rim of the northlands,

Frozen sea—

Where summer's sun never sets

And winter sleeps the longest night.

Here, at the top of the world, time has no zone,

But the white *bear* tramps to the rhythm of freeze and thaw.

Hers is a crystal kingdom of ice fields and blue shadows.

A fractured world of drifting floes.

She knows the language of snow,

The teeth of the blizzard,

The mood of the *walrus*,

The scent of *seal* breath at the melt hole.

She knows vast distance, solitude, and hunger,

Chilling Arctic beauty,

Where the only warmth lies beneath her own thick fur.

Prairie

Old prairie lands that once stretched far
Now lie, precious and few,
Protected from the plow.
Plains of tall bluestem brush the *bison's* shaggy hide.
Gopher and *prairie dog* tunnel beneath sweet buffalo grass
As *pronghorn* graze,
Under the eye of *box turtle*, resting at the creek.
Swelling seed heads sway in the ripening sun,
But, deep in the dark earth, tangled roots lock tight,
As anchor against wild weather.
For on this broad stage, nature plays the drama queen—
Swift in anger to curse with drought,
Blast a scouring wind,
Spin a fury of tornadoes.

Woodland

Who can resist a woodland path
Dressed in changing colors of the year?
Spring casts a spell of wild flowers,
Summer offers cool aisles of dappled green,
Fall blazes great halls of fire, crackling underfoot,
Winter whispers a story of glistening tracks in snow.
Step inside. Explore, clamber, climb.
Probe twisted root and hollow trunk,
Dens of imagination.
But keep watch, listen . . .
Someone slips through the glade,
Something slides among toadstools,
Sips at the mossy bank of the stream.
They see you—shy *deer*, silent *adder*,
crafty, slinking *fox*.

Coral reef

Jewel box of the ocean,
Where gaudy *fish* glint like trinkets in the sparkling blue.
Does the rainbow plunge here,
Splashing color to life as scale and fin?
Polyps wriggle,
Vivid gems of emerald, ruby, and gold,
Building their strange colonies of living rock;
Hideaway for *shrimp* and *crab*,
Refuge for the weary *turtle*.
Who guards your bright treasure?
Not swooping *ray* or skulking *octopus*,
But one who stalks the silver shoals,
Noses nooks and crannies,
Spies the flash of prey in the crusty crevice.
Treacherous *shark*,
He knows the reef is rich with more than splendor.

Desert

Golden Sahara, wide as Africa,
Lies beneath the scorching sun,
Crescents of shifting dunes and rippled sand-seas
Sculpted by the whim of the wind.
All things that move and grow within
Share one dream of water.
Acacia sinks her roots deep at the oasis,
Antelope seeks moisture from leaf and grass,
Viper and *scorpion* burrow away from the heat of noon.
Camel must walk through the fierce day,
Across many burning horizons,
Before she can kneel beside her long shadow and drink,
Knowing another thirsty journey lies ahead.
Parched, arid desert,
Speak your warning that the world may hear,
For sand is creeping toward the green lands.

Rock pool

Now you see it, now you don't,

Little sea, captured by the rocks

As the moon-tugged tide ebbs from the shore.

Nestled among drying boulders studded with limpets,

Rock pool's basin sparkles with the water of life—

A chance of tidbits for the *crystal prawn*,

Prey within reach of *anemone's* grasp,

Safe hunting for the *starfish*,

A hideout of coral weed for *blenny* and *crab*.

But summer's heat and winter's cold trouble a shallow world,

Gull is ever watchful with a hungry eye,

The shimmering peace is brief—

First a splash, then a crash, and tide's turmoil returns.

Nature's precious aquarium:

Now you see it, now you don't.

Mountain

I am the highest mountain,
Born in a collision of continents.
All is beneath me, except the sun, moon, and stars.
I am rock,
Crag, cliff, and ledge, draped in veils of white.
I am snow-maker, with glaciers in my arms,
Whose meltwater swells great rivers below.
My eyes are stealthy *snow leopard*,
Sure-footed *yak*,
Golden eagle, soaring through the pass.
My jaw is a gaping crevasse.
My voice, the roar of avalanche, crack of ice,
Hiss of racing wind.
But in my silence are mysteries of deep time,
Knowledge of more than savage storm
And blue heaven;
For once, an ancient ocean
Left fossils nestling in my bones.

The Outback

Outback flames in the sunset,
Rock glows red as rust.
Across the wide purple plain of blue bush and golden wattle,
Heat rises from the sand.
Watch awhile . . .
Lizard is lazing on the warm bluff, shadows deepen in the gorge,
Kangaroo nuzzles her joey beneath the ghost gum tree.
It's time for *bilby* to peep from his burrow among the hummock grass,
For *cockatoo* to roost,
And *dingo* sniff the air.
Soon, it will be the hour of *boobooks* and *nightjars*,
Soon, a sky of diamonds will sparkle in the billabong.
Hour of the old stories.
For this is a land made in Dreamtime.

Moorland

Moorland, bird land, free as the sky,
Where *lapwing* tumbles through the lively wind,
Curlew calls,
Merlin, the sharp-eyed hunter, stoops and dives.
Moorland, bird land,
Whose purple heather hides the *plover's* chick and nest,
Nurtures *vole*, who feeds the swooping *owl*,
Disguises *grouse*.
Moorland, bird land,
Where mossy bog, reservoir of rain, welcomes the wading *snipe*
To probe his long bill in dark, peaty pools,
Graced by *dragonflies*.
Ragged *sheep* may graze your rolling hills, *fox* patrol the bracken.
Red stag raises his mighty antler crown.
But wind knows
And *skylark* sings—
Wild, free moorland is bird land.

Deep sea

Down, down, down, beyond any glimmer of sunlight
The deep sea stirs.
Black as space, alien as a distant planet.
Realm of *viperfish* and *fangtooth*,
Giant squid, looming and sprawling through endless night.
But all is not hidden in its darkness—
Anglerfish glow with living light to lure their prey,
Jellyfish sparkle,
Shrimp warn with a dazzling flash.
Twinkling ribbons of *siphonophores* drift and swirl
Above the barren seabed, where nothing grows but hunger.
Unpredictable world—
Where *tubeworms* cluster around hot chimneys of poison gas,
Mussels cling to the shores of salt pools.
What unimagined creatures lurk in those depths?
What secrets wait to amaze an explorer's eye?

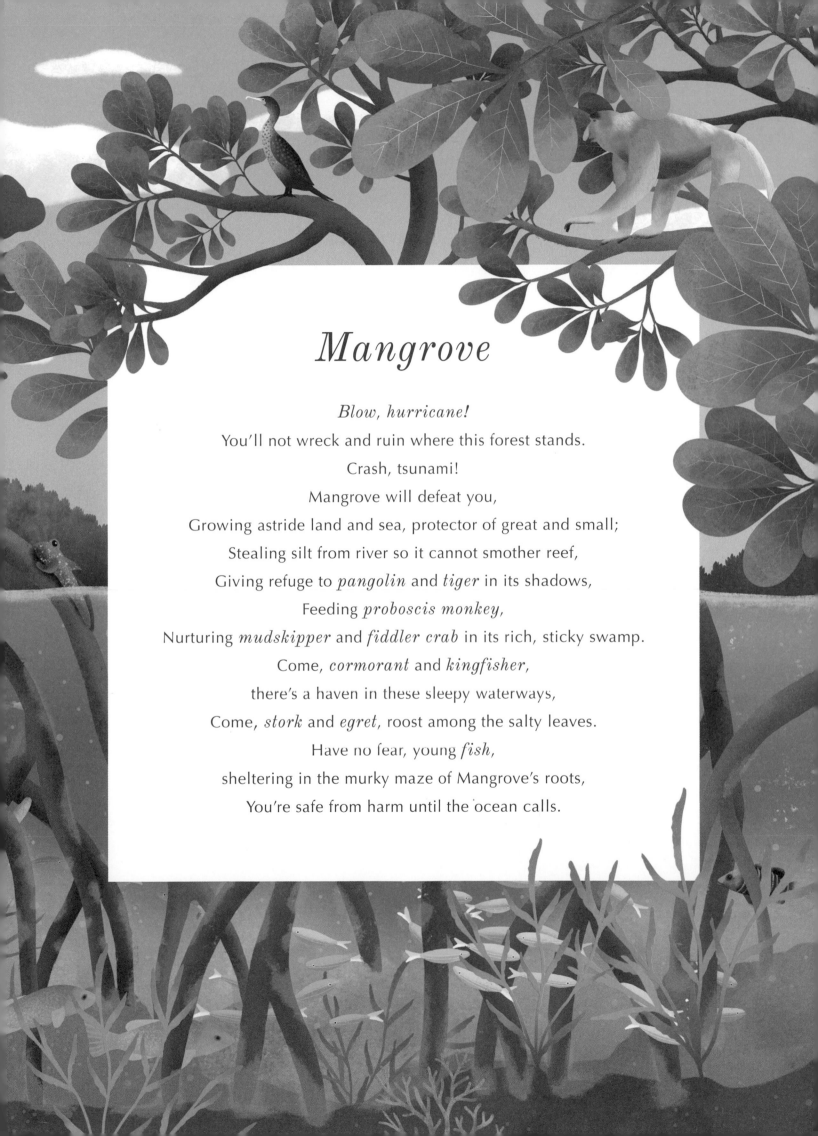

Mangrove

Blow, hurricane!
You'll not wreck and ruin where this forest stands.
Crash, tsunami!
Mangrove will defeat you,
Growing astride land and sea, protector of great and small;
Stealing silt from river so it cannot smother reef,
Giving refuge to *pangolin* and *tiger* in its shadows,
Feeding *proboscis monkey*,
Nurturing *mudskipper* and *fiddler crab* in its rich, sticky swamp.
Come, *cormorant* and *kingfisher*,
there's a haven in these sleepy waterways,
Come, *stork* and *egret*, roost among the salty leaves.
Have no fear, young *fish*,
sheltering in the murky maze of Mangrove's roots,
You're safe from harm until the ocean calls.

Savanna

Savanna speaks in whispering grasses,
In the chatter of *cicadas* across an endless plain.
Spacious homeland of swift *cheetah*
And *gazelle*, with the horizon in her eye.
Kingdom of *lion*, who reigns from the sunbaked rock,
While *elephants* graze among scattered umbrella trees,
Where *giraffes* browse
And *leopard* hides her prey
From scavenging *hyena*.
Yet a fierce roar cannot command the sky.
Lion can only listen for wind, wait for storm clouds
To flood the dry rivers and green the land with fresh, sweet grass,
Remembering Savanna's ancient promise—
That his cubs will grow strong
When *wildebeest* and *zebra* follow the rain.

LEARN MORE ABOUT OUR WILD WORLD . . .

The amazing wild places of the world support an astonishing variety of life,
but human activity is causing damage that threatens wilderness everywhere.

RAIN FOREST

Tropical rain forests cover only 6 percent of the Earth, but are home to over half its plant and animal species. Their tall trees supply oxygen to the planet and soak up carbon dioxide and other greenhouse gases that can cause the planet to warm and so harm the environment. However, every year huge areas are destroyed to make room for farming, or to provide timber.

ARCTIC

This land of ice at the top of the world is important in controlling Earth's temperature because it reflects heat and sunlight back into space. But climate change is causing the Arctic ice to shrink. This is allowing the ocean to absorb more sunlight and become warmer still, reducing habitat for animals and raising sea levels around the world.

PRAIRIE

Prairies are areas of grassland where there is too little rain for trees to grow. Grass roots can reach water several feet below the surface, and anchor soil in storms. Prairies are home to many native insects, plants, and even large mammals such as bison. However, of the 2 million acres of original North American prairie, 99 percent has been turned to farmland.

WOODLAND

Woodland mostly consists of deciduous trees, which lose their leaves in winter. It makes a good home for animals, birds, insects, and plants, but recently has been suffering from increasing numbers of pests and diseases. Rising temperatures, leading to heavier rainfall and droughts, and the invasion of new species also threaten woodland.

CORAL REEF

Coral polyps are tiny, soft-bodied creatures that attach to each other, forming huge reefs over thousands of years. Reef worlds support a quarter of all sea life, but coral cannot survive if the water temperature is too high, and huge areas of reef have been damaged beyond repair due to warming seas. Pollution and destructive fishing also destroy this ancient habitat.

DESERT

The Sahara is the world's largest hot desert, with temperatures reaching up to 120 degrees Fahrenheit during the day. Animals have cleverly adapted to live here, so even small changes in their environment have a big effect. Increasing drought caused by climate change can dry up water holes, while a hotter climate leads to more wildfires that destroy vital trees and shrubs.

ROCK POOL

Coastal areas make up only 10 percent of the sea, but they are home to over 90 percent of its species. Sunlight falls through the shallow waters and encourages plants to grow, which support many sea creatures. But much of the world's tourism takes place here too. Hotels, restaurants, boats, and vacationers create waste, which pollutes the water and causes habitat loss.

MOUNTAIN

The top of Mount Everest is the highest point on Earth. Mountains are formed when two land plates crash into each other, pushing the Earth's crust up high. Global warming is reducing that unique habitat of ice and snow. It is also shrinking glaciers, which feed large rivers below and supply drinking water to many people.

OUTBACK

The outback is the vast, dry area of central Australia. Few people live here, so in general, the natural environment has remained unspoiled, and animals have adapted to its harsh conditions. The outback has always suffered dry spells, but experts think that periods of drought—and extreme weather like tornadoes—will increase in the future because of climate change.

MOORLAND

Three-quarters of the world's heather moorland is found in Great Britain, where it is home to many endangered bird species. The moors appear wild, but many of them were created when woodland was first cleared thousands of years ago. Air pollution and overgrazing have recently damaged the heather, allowing unwelcome grass and scrub to grow.

DEEP SEA

Far below the sea's surface is a world that is little known. 60 percent of the Earth is covered by water over 5,000 feet deep. Without any sunlight, plants cannot grow there, but a huge number of creatures call this dark environment home. However, weighted fishing nets dragged along the seabed and mining for oil cause devastation in this fragile environment.

MANGROVE

Mangrove forests grow on the soft soils of tropical coasts, where they are flooded twice a day by the incoming tide. They are important habitats for fish, providing a nursery among their roots where the young can grow safely. These delicate ecosystems are vulnerable to overfishing, and many mangrove forests have been cleared for farmland, homes, or timber.

SAVANNA

Hot, dry savannas are where you will find some of the world's most famous and beloved animals: the elephant, zebra, and lion. They once roamed freely, but are increasingly losing areas of their homeland to farming. Irrigation for crops has also robbed precious water from the savanna grasses, while dry climate conditions are turning grassland to desert in some places.

HELP TO PROTECT THE WILD WORLD

As you have discovered, our world is in danger. Most of the energy used to make things that we need comes from burning coal, gas, or oil. This pollutes the Earth's atmosphere and is causing our climate to change. Temperatures are rising, permanently melting polar ice and raising sea levels. In some parts of the world, there are long periods of drought, in other parts heavy rain or fierce storms. We can all protect the wild world right now by *using less energy.* You can help by switching off lights when a room is empty, turning off televisions and computers when they're not being used, and walking or biking instead of using a car.

The wild world is also threatened by the trash we throw away. Some is burned, adding to climate change. Some is buried, where it can pollute water in the ground and poison rivers. Some is dumped at sea, killing marine life and littering beaches. You can protect the wild world by *creating less trash.* Learn how to recycle as much as possible; give unwanted clothes, books, and toys to charity; and use rechargeable batteries to save harmful waste.

Some methods of farming, fishing, and forestry damage precious habitats. You can protect the wild world by *choosing carefully what you buy.* Look out for labels that show a product comes from a sustainable source. Choose organic fruit and vegetables, as they've been grown without pesticides, which can pollute rivers, and buy recycled paper to save trees.

The wild world is all around us—in city parks and backyards, as well as the amazing places in this book. We can *protect the wild world* by caring for it close to home. Find out how to feed birds and animals when food is scarce, make safe areas for small mammals to hibernate, build homes for insects, especially bees, and create a new habitat for wildlife by growing a plant or making a garden.

Explore it, protect it, love it.
Our Earth is a wonderful wild world.